I'd Rather be Flying

The Airborne Life and Times of Ted Pearcey

by

Gary Hebbard

I'd Rather be Flying

The Airborne Life and Times of Ted Pearcey

by

Gary Hebbard

CREATIVE PUBLISHERS

St. John's, Newfoundland
2000

THE CANADA COUNCIL | LE CONSEIL DES ARTS
FOR THE ARTS | DU CANADA
SINCE 1957 | DEPUIS 1957

We acknowledge the support of The Canada Council for the Arts for our publishing program.

We acknowledge the financial support of the Government of Canada through the Book Publishing Industry Development Program (BPIDP) for our publishing activities.

Cover: *Summer of 92, Western Labrador* ©Robin LeDrew
from the collection of Dr. Bill Arsenault

∞ Printed on acid-free paper

Published by

CREATIVE BOOK PUBLISHING
a division of 10366 Newfoundland Limited
a Robinson-Blackmore Printing & Publishing associated company
P.O. Box 8660, St. John's, Newfoundland A1B 3T7

Printed in Canada by:
ROBINSON-BLACKMORE PRINTING & PUBLISHING

Canadian Cataloguing in Publication Data

Hebbard, Gary, 1948-
  I'd rather be flying
  Includes bibliographical references and index.
  ISBN 1-894294-20-3

1. Pearcey, Ted.   2. Air pilots — Newfoundland — Biography
3. Aeronautics, Commercial — Newfoundland — History.   I. Title

TL540.P42H43   2000   629.13'092   C00-950102-9

This book is dedicated to my late father,
John A. (Jack) Hebbard (1916-1993)
who never failed to look up at the sound of an
airplane passing and bequeathed that happy trait
to all three of his sons.

LIST OF PHOTOGRAPHS

Ted Pearcey with his mother, Mary (Malone). 11

Ted with American Consul, John Copeland 16

Ted with re-built Piper J-3 Cub 23

Pearcey in co-pilot's seat of ... DC-4 24

CF-NFU and CF-NFV at Piper dealership in Toronto 28

Newfoundland Government Piper Super Cub 33

De Havilland Otter 40

Canso water bomber 44

Ted Pearcey with Premier Smallwood 53

Taking delivery of Beech King Air A100 62

With Bell 206 Ranger purchased by Craig Dobbin 66

Cessna Citation business jet 68

Cockpit of Beech King Air 200 69

Bell 206 Jet Ranger, Executive Helicopters 76

CONTENTS

Foreword ix

Chapter 1 — Emergency Landing   1

Chapter 2 — Early Days   9

Chapter 3 — Growing 15

Chapter 4 — Learning 21

Chapter 5 — Taking Wing 31

Chapter 6 — Gaining Experience 37

Chapter 7 — Advancing 41

Chapter 8 — Maturing 49

Chapter 9 — Government Service 57

Chapter 10 — Parting of the Ways with Government 65

Chapter 11 — Whirlybirds 67

Chapter 12 — Into Business 71

Chapter 13 — Rotary Days 75

Chapter 14 — A Case of Salvage: One More Story 79

Appendix I — List of Aircraft Ted Pearcey Flew 83

Appendix II — Sources 84

Index 85

FOREWORD

The spring of 1989 felt like a real spring. Around the province, from St. John's to Harbour Breton to Port aux Basques to Labrador City, the snow was melting. Literally. And politically.

Politically, the snow was melting for a Conservative administration now led by Tom Rideout. After seventeen years in power, the Conservatives had worn out their welcome with the Newfoundland electorate. They actually edged the Liberals in popular vote, but lost out in seats.

Rideout and the Conservatives had been broadsided by several pieces of bad news — it was revealed Canada had agreed to give northern cod to France in exchange for sending the St. Pierre boundary case to arbitration; the Hibernia project was delayed, again.

I saw this story unfold from a unique vantage point — I followed Tom Rideout for the entire campaign, and had a ring-side seat as the Conservative dream faded.

During that campaign, we helicoptered in and out of communities up and down the Newfoundland coastline. Our guide, and pilot, was the legendary Ted Pearcey. I had heard of his reputation as a pilot of unequalled talent, but until the political spring, I had never met the man.

Ted Pearcey was all I had heard, and more. What impressed me most about his flying was not the flying itself. It was the care he showed for all of us on board. He cautioned us that when we left the helicopter, that we duck until well out of range of its still-turning blades. While we were in the air, he was concerned that the pilot of a helicopter carrying a second party of reporters and political assistants, not travel over water. Into our headsets, he would tell us the second pilot was flying too low.

Gary Hebbard has captured the spirit of a man who is not only a flyer, but a pioneer in the development of aviation in Newfoundland. I'm happy I had the chance to fly in his caring company.

—Doug Letto
Paradise
April 2000

The Author Thanks:

First and foremost, I offer my sincerest thanks to Mr. Ted Pearcey, an uncommon man who flies through life with extraordinary confidence. Ted gave up many hours of his time to relate the facts that form the basis of this book. I thank him not only for his courtesy during the process but for the faith he displayed in choosing me as his Boswell. I am grateful for the opportunity.

Former MHAs Bill Callahan and Tom Hickey were courteous and helpful in sharing their memories, bringing an added richness to the text that would have otherwise been lacking. Bill Callahan, in a later incarnation as managing editor of The Telegram, plucked the author from chronic under-employment in the belief he could be taught to string words together into recognizable news stories. Thanks, Bill.

Creative Book Publishing and particularly Don Morgan, general manager, deserve special thanks for trusting a — to them — unknown quantity who *said* he had a story to tell.

Ken Simmons, Associate News Editor of The Telegram and a good friend. Simple thanks hardly seem adequate. His forte is the deft smoothing of rough edges, an area in which the author provided plenty of scope for his talents. 'Preciate it, man.

To *Telegram* senior photographer Keith Gosse, Michelle Hebbard and the folks at Newfoundland Camera Imaging Centre, thanks for the Kodak moments.

And always to my wife, Beverly, and my children, Paul and Pamela, my undying love and devotion. They shape who I am.

They provide my greatest joy in life.

Chapter 1

Emergency Landing

The date was August 11, 1975 and for the first and only time in his career Ted Pearcey was about to bend an airplane entrusted to his care.

The Beechcraft King Air 100 bearing registration C-FGNL was built by Beech Aircraft in Wichita, Kansas, in 1973 and carries serial number B 184. In that same year it was bought and imported into Canada by the Government of Newfoundland and Labrador, hence the last three letters of the registration.

Takeoff that summer day from runway 29 at St. John's airport was normal. With Pearcey in the cockpit of GNL was co-pilot Charlie Goobie and seated in the comfortable cabin, designed to carry up to eight, were just two passengers — government cabinet ministers Tom Hickey and Joe Rousseau. They were headed to the west coast on government business and the intended destination was Deer Lake airport. The flight took approximately eighty minutes and was routine until, on final approach to the runway, Pearcey called for "gear down" and Goobie pulled the handle used to lower the wheels for landing.

1

"The gear made a sound like it was going down," Pearcey remembers clearly, "but we got a blinking light on the instrument panel indicating unsafe. So we did an overshoot (abandoning the landing and circling the airport) and levelled off and tried it again a number of times and tried circuit breakers and went through the whole emergency procedure."

The landing gear, with a wheel at the nose and one under each wing, refused all attempts to make it fully deploy and lock securely into position so it would carry the full weight of the plane on touchdown. Repeated recycling — attempting to raise and lower it — failed. Trying to eyeball the problem from the cockpit and the passenger compartment got them nowhere so, notifying the airport tower of the problem, Pearcey was told to make a low pass so observers could get a clear look. They could see the nose gear, which retracted in a rearward direction, extended to an angle of about forty-five degrees and stuck in that position while the main wheels were fully extended but not locked, flapping around like broken limbs in the aircraft's slipstream.

"So, I had to make a decision. What am I going to do," said Pearcey.

A reasonable question, but one that Pearcey was well qualified to answer. Pearcey had been taken with the lure of aviation from a very young age and had found himself holding a responsible, though non-flying, job in the industry by the time he was twenty. After acquiring his private pilot's license in 1953 he'd amassed thousands of hours as the pilot in command of a wide variety of aircraft. Flying the bush in Labrador, delivering mail to coastal Newfoundland communities, ferrying the sick to hospital, scientists on their projects, water to douse raging forest fires, passengers to their destinations and politicians to their constituents had exposed Pearcey to virtually every facet of flight and the myriad curve balls it can throw at those who choose to make their living in the air.

From a mechanical point of view, pulling over to the side of the road and poking around under the hood wasn't an option and it was growing ever more likely that a safe conclusion was going to boil down to Pearcey's skill as what pilots call a "stick and rudder man," his ability to make the aircraft do what *he* wanted it to. But none of this obtruded itself on his conscious mind as Pearcey sought a solution to the dilemma. Years of training and hard-won instinct came into play without being deliberately summoned by a mind already evaluating every option.

These included a belly landing at Deer Lake, where emergency facilities weren't as good as those at St. John's; flying on to Gander, where emergency facilities were better: or return all the way to St. John's where, in addition to adequate emergency services was the added advantage of the government hanger, the airplane's home base, with its staff of expert engineers and mechanics, trained in all the systems of the King Air.

It didn't take long for Pearcey to decide that St. John's was the best option. With a sincere wish for a safe landing, Deer Lake air radio gave clearance for the return flight to the capital city. The protruding landing gear, causing additional drag on the otherwise clean airframe, slowed the return flight but otherwise it was routine. About three hours after departing St. John's for Deer Lake, GNL was approaching St. John's airport.

As the stricken craft drew closer to its final destination, Pearcey had been able to contact both the St. John's control tower to advise them of his problem and the government maintenance personnel at hanger 3. This allowed him to discuss with the trained professionals the best way to handle the crisis. With about ninety minutes fuel remaining, Pearcey and Goobie had plenty of time to circle the city at a safe altitude while they considered all their options for what increasingly looked like a wheels-up emergency landing. Discussion with those on the ground continued.

"So I said, in the event of a landing without wheels, I'd like to find out from Beech what the recommended procedure is. So they got on the phone to Beech and they said keep the power on right until touchdown (for maximum control) because you don't know for sure if the gear is going to collapse or what."

But Pearcey disagreed. The pilot of a plane in flight, like the captain of a ship at sea, is the final authority when it comes to decisions affecting the safety of his craft and passengers. The pilot is, after all, the person at the pointy end. But with that authority, of course, goes ultimate responsibility. Get it wrong and you can expect to bear the full blame for your decisions.

After careful consideration, Pearcey was convinced that keeping the engines running at high power until the plane impacted the runway was too dangerous for several reasons. For one, the propellers of a King Air are located on each wing adjacent to the cockpit and roughly in line with the lower extremities of the pilot and co-pilot. Their sudden impact with the runway while operating at high power could shatter the spinning blades, turning them into lethal shrapnel. Flying pieces of prop could also puncture the fuel tanks in the wings, causing a fire and the sudden stoppage of the engines when the props hit the ground would very likely tear the engines from their mounts, causing still more damage and danger. But most important of all, high-octane aviation fuel would still be flowing to both engines, and the electrical system operating. That greatly increased the risk of fire.

With these thoughts in mind, Pearcey determined that if all efforts to fix the landing gear failed and a crash landing was inevitable, he would cut all fuel and electricity to the engines before impact in an effort to minimize damage, and decrease the risk of fire.

An overflight of the St. John's control tower confirmed the main wheels were still flopping uselessly below the wing while the nose wheel protruded in an ungainly attitude. Low passes were made over the government hanger so engineers could eyeball the problem while discussions by radio continued. It soon became obvious that a wheels-up landing was inevitable. With only a bare minimum of fuel remaining in the tanks to maintain control until engine shutdown, Pearcey committed the crippled plane to its final approach.

"I came in a little fast, got over the end of the runway, cut the engines and the props started to go into feather.* But I had extra speed, about ten to fifteen knots above normal touchdown speed of sixty knots so I could control it right down to touchdown. The engines were off, the fuel mixture and electrics were cut and everything before we touched the runway. As we touched I could feel something hit the ground, but we were lower than we usually were because as the weight came on the gear it just folded up ... but not all the way up."

Despite the engines being shut down, the props continued to turn although they were not under power and were slowing quickly. The awkward angle of the stuck nose gear now became a blessing in disguise. It kept the nose up just high enough to keep the engines from hitting the ground,

---

* Without power the prop blades automatically turn their edges into the wind to reduce drag, a condition called feathering.

although at least one blade on each propeller was bent backwards. The rear of the plane settled, the fuselage touching just aft of the exit door near the tail.

Just prior to touchdown Pearcey had briefed the passengers on what was happening and how to brace themselves, making sure also that they were securely belted in.

"So I told them that as soon as I yelled to take off their belts and the co-pilot would be back there with them sitting opposite the cabin door and as soon as we came to a stop on the runway he would open the door and push it out and he'd run out. 'As soon as you see him leave the aircraft, you follow him,' " Pearcey instructed.

"The aircraft settled down with just a scraping and grinding and no engine power on. We had very little fuel left because of all the time we'd spent circling the airport," Pearcey recalled.

In an amazingly short distance the plane slid to a halt in a spectacular shower of sparks and dust. As soon as it stopped, Goobie opened the rear door and ran out, followed closely by two shaken but unhurt cabinet ministers. Pearcey evacuated the cockpit as quickly as possible and was the last one out. In the meantime, the airport crash trucks were roaring up to the smoking wreck and one of them almost ran down Rousseau.

"As we were going out behind the wing where the passenger door is located Joe Rousseau was running," Pearcey said, beginning to chuckle at the memory. "And the driver puts his head out the window and says to Joe: 'Lard Jesus buddy, are you trying to get yourself killed?' I thought it was the funniest thing, afterwards."

Rousseau has since died but Tom Hickey lives today in St. John's where he owns and operates a nightclub. He remembers the incident vividly and bursts out laughing when recalling Rousseau's death-defying dash out of the crashed plane and nearly into the path of the emergency vehicle. Of course it could have been serious, he concedes, even fatal, but at the time it seemed to add just the right touch of the absurd to a situation that was otherwise unrelentingly grim.

He also recalls Pearcey's efforts to find and fix the problem with the landing gear while Goobie circled the airport. The effort entailed much scrabbling around in the belly of the plane, leaving Pearcey smeared with dirt and grease. Hickey had removed his beige coloured sports jacket in the comfortable atmosphere of the pressurized, air-conditioned cabin and laid it on an unused seat. Somehow Pearcey came in accidental contact with it, leaving a greasy hand print on one shoulder. Nobody noticed it at the time or, given the circumstances, would have cared. Hickey donned the jacket before the landing and shortly after getting clear of the wreckage he was speaking with an RCMP officer who was at the scene.

"And he said, 'Mr. Hickey you've got a big grease stain here on the back of your jacket,' and I said, 'oh, that's just Rousseau in a hurry to get out trying to jump over me,'" quipped Hickey.

Rousseau immediately joined in the gale of laughter that swept the crowd gathered on the runway and what could have been a far more tense moment was put into its proper context.

Why didn't Pearcey put the aircraft down on the seemingly softer grass along side the runway instead of the hard and unforgiving pavement? He had a ready response: he'd considered it, he said, and even discussed it with those on the ground. But he chose the asphalt because he knew, from walking it in the past, that the earth beneath the deceptively smooth grass covering was so rough and uneven it could easily send the skidding, unpowered plane out of control. In the final event the crippled plane slid only a few hundred feet in a near-perfect straight line down the runway before coming to a safe stop. The flaps were torn off, propeller blades bent and some body panels scratched and buckled but overall the damage was minimal.

"I thought it was one of my better landings," Pearcey laughed. "But there was a hell of a scraping noise because there was no roaring engine noise with the power off."

And, as he'd anticipated, as the props touched the runway the blades just bent backwards rather than shattering. The damaged aircraft was quickly retrieved from the runway by the government maintenance crews, taken to hanger 3 for repair and was soon back in service.

Today the aircraft, still looking sharp in its distinctive overall white with orange and brown striping, has been specially fitted out as a flying hospital room and can be seen coming and going from airstrips around the province in the role of air ambulance, transporting the sick or injured to hospital. Later investigation determined the entire problem was caused by contamination of the hydraulic fluid in the actuator mechanism that operates the landing gear. Unlike many other types of aircraft, the King Air B100 undercarriage at that time was, according to Pearcey, set up so that the entire mechanism was controlled by the nose gear. When it failed to extend fully, the remainder of the system was crippled. The system on later model King Airs was changed.

As for Pearcey, he took the incident in stride.

"I didn't dwell on it."

Chapter 2

Early Days

Like most fourteen-year-old boys, Ted Pearcey's imagination wasn't a thing easily shackled. Certainly not by anything as mundane and dreary as the dusty confines of a school room, even one run by the notoriously strict Christian Brothers at Holy Cross School on Patrick Street in St. John's, Newfoundland during the third year of World War Two.

The first half of 1942 had yet to see the change in the fortunes of the Allied nations that would eventually lead to the full and final victory over the forces of German Naziism, Italian Fascism and Japanese bushido in 1945. But it was getting closer and there were hopeful signs, among them the Hurricane fighter planes of 125 Squadron, 1 Group of the RCAF, stationed at Torbay airport just north of the city. Less technologically advanced than the more glamorous Spitfire, the Hurricane was still a sleek and deadly front-line fighting machine with its eight (sometimes twelve) wing-mounted machine guns — just the sort of argosy to carry away the fancy of a young school boy from the incessant drone of earthbound lessons. The planes performed any number of duties over and around the Avalon Peninsula, including patrolling the sea lanes off the coast for signs of German submarines. It was the stuff of every young boy's dreams of adventure and heroism. But the sudden impact of an unerringly aimed piece of chalk just above the left ear could, and did, break the spell, drawing attention back to reality with sudden, painful finality.

"There was one Christian Brother there, Billy Stoyles," Pearcey reminisces nearly six decades later in his comfortable home just outside St. John's. "... if you had a fly on your forehead, he could hit that fly with a piece of chalk if he wanted to. He never missed my head. I'd be sitting there by the wall gazing out the window (at fleeting Hurricanes) and BANG, he's hit me right there (pointing to a spot just above his left ear). He'd never miss."

There was no malice in Stoyles' target practice, Pearcey is quick to add. It was just another in the bag of tricks an experienced teacher used to effectively reclaim the attentions of a daydreaming teenager whose proper place, body and spirit, was the classroom.

"He never said much," Pearcey fondly recalled of Stoyles. "He'd just laugh."

That piece of chalk, as likely as not, was the defining event to that point in Pearcey's young life, a dim and not yet fully formed awareness that his future would lay somewhere in the clean sky above the dusty roadways of St. John's. To this day Pearcey can close his eyes and see again with perfect clarity the nimble Hurricanes, flitting like insects around a gunnery target being towed sedately by a plodding utility aircraft over the South Side Hills. As each plane would make its practice firing run at the long fabric sleeve streamed by the plane, sharply defined tendrils of smoke would spring dramatically from the guns of the attacking fighter, stitching a pattern of white chevrons across the blue sky.

"You could even hear them if you were outside," Pearcey recalls, "the staccato bang-bang-bang-bang. I was fascinated by that. They'd go by the target and they'd pull up (describing a graceful arc with his hands above his head). It was fantastic."

But the road to professional pilot was to be a long one for young Ted. Indeed, looking at his upbringing, one can legitimately wonder at his eventual career path, youthful enthusiasm notwithstanding. The youngest of nine children, Ted was born to Newfoundland Railway employee William John Pearcey and Mary Elizabeth (Malone) at 68 Hayward Ave. on March 4, 1928. He completed a family of three girls and five other boys. His father was a chief engineer on the coastal boats then owned by the Newfoundland Railway, notably the *Home*, although he also served on the *Kyle*, *Glencoe* and the *Clyde*. During the summer, engineer Pearcey would take his youngest son on his voyages and the remainder of the family would live in Argentia, where the *Home* was based, as she travelled the ports and harbours of Placentia Bay.

"Years afterward, in the sixties, when I was flying I used to wonder what that wreckage was beached at Jersey Har-

Ted Pearcey at age fourteen with his mother, Mary (Malone), taken in 1942.

T. Pearcey collection

bour on the south coast. And I found out this was the *Home*. You can see the remains of it now ... there on its side, all rusty," Pearcey recalls.

His oldest brother, Charles, followed in their father's footsteps, only to be lost in the sinking of the *Caribou* by a German submarine in Cabot Strait on the night of October 14, 1942.

"He was on watch down in the engine room when she was torpedoed and was lost," Pearcey says simply, still obviously affected by the wartime tragedy nearly sixty years in the past. Nor had tragedy finished with the Pearcey family. William was walking back to the *Home*, berthed at Argentia one night in 1945, after a pleasant night visiting ashore. He was stricken by a sudden and massive heart attack as he was boarding the vessel and fell into the water between the ship and the dock.

"Six o'clock the next morning the second engineer, who was working down in the engine room, came up for 'a blow' and leaned on the rail looking down, and here was my father, floating face down. His (uniform) hat was still on and his coat still over his arm," Pearcey related.

The macabre incident left a lifelong impression on the seventeen-year-old son.

But that tragedy lay in the future when Ted was a student at Holy Cross School and, like so many of his contemporaries, he would go off to a movie every Saturday at the Capitol or Star, York or the Nickel theatre and thrill to the newsreels filled with war footage. And of course there were plenty of Hollywood war movies and government propaganda films. During those years Pearcey and two close friends, Bill Kieley and Herb Barnes (since deceased) would eagerly devour each new newspaper report of the great air battles over Europe and the Pacific, learning all about the various types of planes being used by the combatants.

"We knew the speed, what engine power was in every aircraft during the war," Pearcey recalls.

By this time Pearcey's father had purchased one of the houses built for Newfoundland Railway employees on Old Topsail Road. Ted's time away from school was often spent building model planes of balsa wood and doped tissue paper that were then hung around his room in the snug home. His father's untimely death in 1945 put an end to this period of young Ted's life, leaving him at home with his mother and one older sister. Life insurance and a pension made sure Mary Elizabeth and her two children still at home were financially secure but Ted felt it was time he began to make his own way in the world. His formal education ended late in 1945 and, like his father and brother before him, Ted went to work for the railway.

Chapter 3

Growing

The railway express office was Ted's introduction to the working world, handling freight and doing paperwork.

"We'd check in the packages, weigh them and make up the bill of lading for them, that kind of stuff, and when we closed up at five o'clock and the train had left, we'd have to do all of the accounting," he remembers of that first adult job.

For about two years he was content, but for a bright young man with some high school education, at a time when that accomplishment raised one above the common herd, there were lots of interesting things to do, places to go and people to meet.

One of those people was a young man about his own age who worked at the American Consulate on Water Street, around where the Hong Kong Bank of Canada stands today. Ted and this youth, whose name has long since receded into the mists of time, would run into each other every morning when at the post office retrieving their employers mail. One day this new friend told him of a vacancy for an assistant to the vice-consul, a man named John Copeland. Since it paid more than he was then making at the railway and carried

Ted (left) with American Consul John Copeland (centre) and two of the consu-late's female employees, Mary LeValliant (rear) and Corrine Blandin. Circa 1946.

with it the hint of possible travel and adventure, Ted applied and was hired.

Pearcey's memory of that period conjures up the desk he occupied in the waiting room outside Copeland's office. The vice-consul had the authority to issue or extend visas to people in pre-confederation Newfoundland who were travelling to the U.S., but it was Ted they'd encounter on first entering the office.

"So they would come to me and I'd get their paperwork all ready ... and I'd say, 'OK, fine, the vice-consul will be right with you.' I had a chair by my desk and a couple in front of it for people to sit and this guy came in one day. He was a Dane and his name was Henning Reinhold and he wanted to get his visa renewed or updated because he had to go to the States. He was working in Gander as the manager of Scandi-navian Airways System (SAS)."

When Ted learned the man's occupation, the conversation — predictably — turned to aviation and it ended some little time later with Reinhold offering Ted a job with SAS in Gander as an assistant dispatcher.

"It wasn't more than a week that I drummed up the $8 to get to Gander by air from Torbay," Pearcey remembered.

He spent a weekend, late in 1948, being shown over the SAS operation in Gander. The following spring he took the job when the incumbent left and found himself at last in the world of aviation that had first called to him as a school boy. It wasn't glamorous work, meeting arriving aircraft in all kinds of weather, directing them into their parking spots, greeting passengers and leading them into the terminal building, doing the calculations of weights and balances as freight, passengers and fuel were added to or removed from the planes, and a hundred other small but important tasks. Still, despite this daily immersion in things aviation, the idea of piloting one of the machines he so slavishly serviced had yet to take root.

At this time there was only one privately owned plane kept at Gander airport, a de Havilland Tiger Moth biplane owned by Jack Janes, later to become Gander's well known and long-serving airport manager. Jack wasn't really a pilot in those days, Pearcey recalls. He'd get an experienced pilot to go with him when he wanted to fly somewhere, handling the controls under the professional's watchful eye.

One of these obliging men was an experienced American pilot who worked for one of the other airlines that had offices in Gander. He and Ted met and one day Ted found himself aloft in Jack Janes' Tiger Moth, doing a few loops and rolls. He was enthraled. Ted would fly with this man, his name long forgotten, only a few times but more than enough to whet his appetite for more.

In this way Pearcey's head remained in the clouds, and

his luck held when he made the acquaintance of Ian Dunlop, a dispatcher for British Overseas Airways Corporation (BOAC) who had his own plane, a Taylorcraft, with seating for only the pilot and one passenger, a 65 h.p. engine and a tiny tail wheel. Taking the controls when flying with Dunlop, Ted finally got to feel what it was like to actually guide a plane through the air, making it respond to his commands.

"I guess for a year or so I was flying around with Dunlop every once in a while. He gave me a lot of tips but I never did get to sit in the left (pilot's) seat," he recalled.

Dunlop was soon transferred back to England and, unable to take it with him, sold the little Taylorcraft to Ted and two friends for $1,200. Now it remained only for them to find someone to teach them to fly their new toy.

The calendar now showed 1952 and Ted had left SAS for a more responsible job at Pan American Airways (PAA) doing flight planning for aircraft passing over Gander on their way to Europe. He'd gather all the latest relevant weather information the pilots of an approaching plane would need to decide on a transAtlantic crossing, and plot it out for them on a map. He would relay the information to them by radio and, if the pilots were satisfied the weather was suitable, they would overfly Gander and carry on. If not, they would land and refuel, sometimes waiting for better weather or more favourable winds before heading out over the unforgiving north Atlantic.

Enter now Ted Henley, former World War Two bomber pilot, future businessman, actor, civil servant, story teller extraordinaire, man-about-town and Newfoundland icon who was then Ted's boss at Pan Am as chief dispatcher and, later, station manager. He'd flown combat missions with the RAF during the war and then taught flying to new recruits and when Ted and his friends approached him for flying lessons he readily agreed.

Now twenty-four, Pearcey was firmly launched into the blue that would become his professional home. Henley would leave a lasting impression, regaling his students with rousing stories of his own flying experiences.

"He was fascinating, you know. He was very capable, very highly thought of by me. He would talk generally about some of the funny things that happened to him. He never mentioned to me any tragic incidents. He might have mentioned that when he was flying bombers maybe fifty would leave on a mission and only forty of them would get back, stuff like that. What he was interested in was flying procedures and how they developed. When a new type of aircraft would come to a squadron the operational pilots themselves would figure out the best way to fly it to get the best speed out of it while carrying the maximum load and other technical and operational procedures. That was very interesting to me."

Chapter 4

Learning

*H*attie Bragg came into Ted's life in 1950. A native of Port Union, she was then secretary to the Gander manager for American Overseas Airways (AOA). The two were soon married and moved into an apartment. They would have two children together: Debbie Cooper, now a wife, mother and journalist for CBC Television in St. John's and Glen, husband, father, and the training and proficiency check pilot for Canadian Helicopters in Newfoundland. He is stationed in Deer Lake.

Back in the air, Ted's training continued. He made his first solo flight on February 7, 1953, his first cross-country flight (necessary for a private pilot license) on October 21, 1953 and was awarded his private license — # QMP2782 — a month later. (It would not be until October 1961 that Ted obtained his commercial license, permitting him to legally carry passengers for hire.) But even with his private license now nestled snugly in his wallet, Pearcey still had not settled on a career as a professional pilot. In the meantime, his job with Pan Am continued to claim his time and attention, a circumstance that would continue until late 1954. One of the benefits of the job was the opportunity it offered to get to know a wide range of people in the aviation community, especially with the many airlines that then flew through Gander. Then, as now, networking can be the most important part of a growing career — a fact proven when Pearcey met the chief navigator for the Flying Tiger Line.

Through work on his flight plan for the next stage of his trip, he and Pearcey became friends. One day this man announced he was leaving for Europe because Flying Tiger was adding tourist charters to its existing cargo-carrying business, and was going to set up headquarters at Rhein-Main airport in Frankfurt, Germany.

"To make a long story short, he said 'you know, you're quite capable of doing that job. Would you like to go over there and set up our operation, hire the people that you want and operate all over Europe, wherever our charter flights are going?' "

Not surprisingly, Pearcey snatched the opportunity and soon found himself in Germany. Initially, his young family stayed behind in Gander. A bonus to Pearcey's new job was the chance to build up some flight time on his new pilot's license, as his duties frequently required him to fly to a number of European airports to make preparations to handle an incoming Flying Tiger flight. To get around efficiently he would beg, borrow or rent a small plane at every chance. In this way his log book soon boasted flights as pilot in command on the Cessna 172, Aeronca Champ, Piper J-3 Cub, and other small, single-engine planes.

And so, for two years Pearcey travelled most of Europe, slowly but surely — like most people who find themselves in such jobs — becoming jaded by the unrelenting travel. Despite having his family comfortably installed in a lovely old house on a nice street in the German city of Frankfurt, he

T. Pearcey collection

A proud Ted Pearcey poses next to a Piper J-3 Cub that he and a friend bought and rebuilt after it had been damaged in an accident. The picture was snapped in 1955 at Gander Airport.

began to entertain the idea of moving on. But circumstances beat him to it and the entire tourist carrying project was cancelled by Flying Tiger on financial and administrative grounds late in 1956. Pearcey quickly found himself back in Newfoundland, only to once again take advantage of the networking so common in just about any industry, hooking up with a Canadian company, Maritime Central Airways, that stationed him in Montreal for most of the next two years.

"Carl Burke was the owner of it and I met him over in Germany. They wanted to get into the DC-4 (aircraft) to carry

Ted Pearcey in the co-pilot's seat of a Flying Tiger Lines DC-4 on the way to Germany in the mid-fifties.

tourists. Anyway, I ended up going to Montreal and Carl Burke hired me to set up his operation using DC-4s across the Atlantic to all over Europe because of my background."

A couple of years later, 1959 found Ted with Trans Ocean Airline, a company based in Oakland, California. It was operating Boeing 377 Stratocruisers, a large, double-decked aircraft capable of carrying 55 to 112 passengers, out of three different airports on both civilian and military contracts.

"And I was the representative to meet the flights and make sure that they were being handled properly. I was the co-ordinator," Pearcey explained.

The job entailed travelling among three California airports so, again in the name of efficiency, the company assigned him a Cessna 182 from their flying school fleet. At the time of getting checked out in this plane he'd logged about 200 hours as pilot in command.

"I'd get out to Oakland Airport early in the morning and maybe have to fly up to Travis Air Force Base for an arrival up there and turn it around for departure and then maybe come back and stop in at San Francisco and do the same thing there. It was a whole day just going in a triangle."

Occasionally, when time permitted, Pearcey would be able to land at a small airstrip in the wine-soaked Napa Valley for a meal. A pleasant interlude that, like so many good things, was too good to last. Soon a transfer sent Pearcey, family in tow, to the company's base in Chicago, a journey made by car. The job there was the same as back in warm, sunny California — mostly minus the warm, sunny part — but after a few months this job, too, fizzled out and by the end of the year he was back in Newfoundland. His log book now showed a total of 260 flight hours.

Flying jobs in the aviation industry as the 1950s drew to a close, especially in Newfoundland, were scarce and Pearcey, for lack of an aviation job, took a position with Newfoundland Armature Works. He was hired by manager Charlie Dearin as a sort of bill collector, visiting people who owed the company money and attempting to collect payment.

"It was a real fancy job," Pearcey laughed, "in name."

But the pull of the air remained strong, often strengthened by frequent visits to what was then Torbay Airport. In those days, recalled Pearcey, there was still a military presence on the east side of the field, complete with military-style checkpoint on RCAF Road. Having been passed through this barrier, he'd accomplish whatever errand had brought him there with the added bonus of a chance to poke around the hangers. Without the financial means to rent a plane, Pearcey cast about for some way to keep his flying skills honed, eventually hitting on the idea of starting a flying club.

A little poking around revealed there was a military-owned building opposite the guardhouse on RCAF Road that would soon be empty and surplus to military needs. Having been mostly out of the province since 1949, Pearcey lacked a network of local contacts so, in an effort to reach like-minded people, he took out a small ad in *The* (then) *Evening Telegram* asking anyone interested to come to a meeting. It was early 1960.

"A hundred people showed up. And a guy sitting right up in front was a fellow by the name of Bill English who was a school teacher at St. Pat's Hall and his wife's name was Maude." Pearcey remembered.

The meeting was a great success, with most people staying on after it was adjourned to kick around what had been discussed in more detail. The first step, they decided, was to make arrangements to actually take possession of the building Pearcey had singled out, then being used as a warehouse. They eventually succeeded but found themselves with what was basically an empty shell bearing no obvious resemblance at all to a club house. Renovations became the order of the day, Pearcey and English doing the lion's share of the work with occasional help from friends and potential club members.

"I remember we spent a whole winter building, renovating, putting a floor in, putting in walls ... and building in a bar. When we got it pretty well ready to go as a building able to accommodate people, a number of people indicated they wanted to become not full-fledged flying members but associate or social members and it was the bar that brought them in. We used to sell memberships," Pearcey recalled, "and, in fact, the club got off to an excellent start and was soon bringing in revenue."

But what's a flying club without flying machines? It quickly became evident that it was time to start thinking seriously about obtaining some aircraft. From the outset, Pearcey let it be known that in his opinion it would be best to equip themselves with at least two brand new planes rather than used ones, avoiding the many possible pitfalls of dealing with older machines. And it would be far more cost efficient, he insisted, from the maintenance and expense points of view if both machines were the same type.

"I wanted to have uniformity and if we could get new aircraft, that would be the answer."

In July 1961 Pearcey and RCAF pilot/flight instructor Bill Monkman, then stationed in St. John's, travelled to Hamilton, Ontario where they picked up two brand new Piper PA-22 Colts, registered CF-NFU and CF-NFV. The no-frills, low-cost planes each had only two seats, side by side, but with the refinement of a tricycle landing gear, offered easier ground handling than the more complex techniques of the old "taildragger" configuration. With its 108 h.p. Lycoming 0-23-C18 flat four engine, the little craft had a respectable maximum speed of 120 m.p.h. (200 km/h) at sea level and a range with full fuel tanks of 690 miles (almost 1,200 km). Over 1,800 of these aerial sprites were turned out by Piper in just three years of production.

New planes in hand, Pearcey and Monkman left Hamilton on July 3, 1961. Monkman flew NFV while Pearcey was at the controls of NFU. Rest and refuelling stops at Kingston, Ontario, Cartierville and Quebec City, P.Q. Fredericton and Moncton, N.B. were behind them when they arrived in Sydney, N.S. on July 5. Next day they lifted off for Gander, arriving without incident. But the last leg of the journey to St. John's was to be delayed.

CF-NFU and CF-NFV at the Piper dealership in Toronto, 1961. Pearcey, right, stands next to Bill Monkman.

People old enough to remember it will recall the summer of 1961 as one of the worst on record in the province for forest fires. At one point even the South Side Hills of St. John's were aflame and there was much concern for the fate of the oil and gas storage tanks located there. In central Newfoundland, huge tracts of forest from Gambo to the coast at Gander Bay were going up in smoke and when, on July 7, Pearcey and Monkman took off for St. John's the hot, smoke-filled air created conditions dangerous enough to a small plane to convince the two fliers to return to Gander airport to await better conditions. The air cleared a little overnight and takeoff the next day, the ensuing flight and arrival in the capital city were uneventful.

With two brand new airplanes and a viable flying club to support them, NFU and NFV were soon in the air, carrying sightseers, weekend pilots, students and potential students.

According to Pearcey's dog-eared log book, the first passenger to experience the new planes was one Ralph Moore. Exactly who Mr. Moore was, where he was from and other bits of historical detail were not recorded. But others were, and among those to enjoy a sightseeing trip were Ted's late brother, Aiden, an unidentified CJON reporter, Ted's children, Richard Cashin (later of Fishermen's Union fame) and others.

Things were going well, but within a year the St. John's Flying Club was to lose two of its major assets — NFV would be destroyed in an accident near Clarenville while being flown by a student on a cross-country flight, fortunately without serious injury — and Ted Pearcey would go from amateur to professional pilot. It was 1962 and Eastern Provincial Airways had come calling.

Chapter 5

Taking Wing

*M*ost people today who think of the late, lamented Eastern Provincial Airways recall mostly the sleek Boeing 737 passenger jets in their distinctive red and white livery with black lettering. But those old enough to remember back to the late 1940s know that EPA started out small — very small. The fledgling company's first airplane was a war surplus Cessna Crane T-50, a low-wing, twin-engine craft originally used as a military trainer. EPA employed it as a passenger carrier with indifferent success. It would be replaced by more modern equipment, although other war surplus and war era aircraft would serve a number of roles for the operation with great distinction.

In May of 1962 the Newfoundland government purchased two brand new Piper Super Cubs to be used by the forestry department, then also responsible for wildlife management. Lacking any infrastructure to support even this small aerial contingent, the government contracted with EPA to operate and maintain the planes out of a small base on Octagon Pond just west of St. John's in the community of Paradise. Provincial wildlife biologist and caribou specialist

Stuart Peters had done some flight training during the war and was a frequent visitor to the flying club where he and Pearcey became friends and flying companions.

"We got to know each other pretty well," Pearcey remembers, "and he said to me one day 'what do you plan to do, pursue aviation (as a career)?' I said 'yeah, but right now I'm just building up some flying time. I'm not going anyplace.' "

Thus did another friendship lead to another offer, this time for a real flying job. Peters, who later became the deputy minister of forestry, put Pearcey in touch with Royal Cooper, then EPA chief pilot, who hired him to fly one of the new Super Cubs. At this point Pearcey had acquired a commercial license but no instrument, multi-engine or night ratings. But since the new job involved all daytime VFR (visual flight rules) flying, that was no impediment. Pearcey soon found himself doing flights all over the island searching for pest infestations, doing wildlife surveys or forest fire spotting. The navigation was rudimentary but the continuous flying built up his hours — and experience — at a great clip. In the first full year of his new job his log book showed 800 total hours in the air as pilot in command. With a fuel endurance of three to three-and-a-half hours and occasional refuelling, the tough little Pipers could easily put in an eight or nine hour work day in good weather. The down side was that jobs would sometimes keep him away from home for days at a time. And while it was steady, interesting work, adventurous wouldn't have been a good description of the daily grind. It was, Pearcey remembers, mostly a question of low and slow while his passenger gathered whatever information they were in search of on that trip. Still, occasionally, the chance of a bit of fun would offer itself and the little Cub could always be called upon to do its part.

Things could be a little uncomfortable in the spartan

One of the two Piper Super Cubs the Newfoundland government purchased in 1962. The planes were handed over to Eastern Provincial Airways who provided all maintenance, fuel and oil, and pilots, and operated the aircraft for the government.

aircraft, especially in winter when the only heat in the cabin came from the engine's exhaust header. Dressing warmly was essential and Pearcey was lucky to pick up a fleece-lined World War Two flying suit that, although warm, was cumbersome. He remembers having to complete all his exterior pre-flight checks on the aircraft before getting into the suit because it was so constricting.

"When you got in the seat, that was it, you strapped in and you stayed there."

Pearcey clearly has a soft spot in his heart to this day for the trusty little Pipers, which he said never suffered from any serious mechanical problems and never necessitated a forced landing. But that didn't mean mishap, even danger, was ever far away.

Pearcey recalls a caribou survey he flew in September of 1962 that could have led to injury or worse. The site was

Victoria Lake, south of Buchans. The caribou would swim across the lake in their hundreds during their annual migration. Wildlife specialist Dr Tom Bergarud thought this time, when the animals were easily approachable as they were slowed by their passage through the water, would be a good time to collect blood and hair samples that he could later analyze to determine the animals' health. It didn't take a lot of persuasion to get Ted to land on the lake and then taxi up to the herd so Bergarud could grapple a swimming caribou with a large shepherd's crook he carried for the purpose, pulling the struggling animal in to the float.

"There were so many animals that they couldn't get away from the airplane fast enough because others were all around them. You could get right in among them," Pearcey recalled vividly decades later.

Bergarud, straddling a float like some later day cowboy, managed to get the crook around a caribou's neck and pull the terrified animal towards him.

"That was going fine but can you imagine a 300 pound animal with its front hooves going like this (pawing the air above his head with his hands, to demonstrate). Bang-O, right down through the float," Pearcey said.

Fortunately the resulting hole was in the top of the float so it wasn't admitting water but Pearcey quickly realized this was a dangerous undertaking. Not only could the plane be severely damaged by a panicked animal but Bergarud was equally at risk from the sharp, flailing hooves. Over his passenger's objections, Pearcey called an immediate halt to the operation.

"He said, 'come on, let's try it again' but I said 'no way,'" Pearcey insisted. "There's no way you could do that on a little aluminum float on a fabric covered plane."

As a direct result of this experiment, boats were used for

all such work in future. Panicked wildlife notwithstanding, Pearcey said he learned a great deal about his chosen profession during this period of intense flying.

"There's so many things that you learn and, if you're lucky, you learn by getting away without having to pay the price of learning." he said.

Another lesson came a few years later when he was flying a Beaver airplane equipped with skis for winter operation. Gunnar Laurel was then a senior pilot for EPA and one day was flying mail to some islands in Notre Dame Bay, landing on the ice. Laurel had been flying an Otter, the larger brother of the Beaver, all day and was getting tired so Pearcey was told to take his Beaver in with a load of mail to help him out.

"It was the first time I'd been to this spot and when I was approaching I could hear Gunnar on the radio just taking off from there so I asked him what the landing conditions were. 'No wind at all,' he said. You'd better land in the longest run you can."

There was no snow on the ice that day, Pearcey recalled, except a small accumulation along the shoreline. He set up to land and made a good touchdown but suddenly realized that without the added friction of snow on the ice, the plane wasn't slowing much as it skidded along the slick surface. "And here I was going down the ice about 30 miles an hour, maybe 20, but the shoreline was coming up fast. So I pumped the flaps down all the way to try and get more drag and that seemed to help a little but the shoreline was still coming up and there was nothing I could do about it. Finally I got so close I just chopped the power because I didn't want to hurt the prop when I hit the trees."

But a tiny rim of snow right on the shoreline saved him, creating just enough extra friction as he hit it to stop the plane inches from the trees, without damage. Later, Pearcey asked

Laurel why he didn't warn him about the treacherously slick ice.

"I thought you knew," he said. "Knew what?" I replied. "Oh he said, you get on (the ice) and when she won't stop you kick full left rudder and give her a burst of power and that will kick the tail around and you'll be going the other way. Then all you have to do is ease on a little power and ease it off gradually until she stops. I thought you knew. Sure everybody knows that."

That's what Pearcey meant by learning and getting away without paying the price.

Chapter 6

Gaining Experience

After a couple of years flying Pipers, Pearcey began taking on heavier iron — Beavers and Otters, the definitive bush planes manufactured by de Havilland Aircraft of Toronto. The change was a gradual one.

Pearcey was considered by EPA staff, as a result of his flying the provincial government's Super Cubs, to be the "government" pilot, and was therefore trained on new types of aircraft as the government acquired them. Pearcey remembers receiving his Beaver checkout from EPA chief pilot Royal Cooper.

"I can remember that he gave me some touch and goes (landings and takeoffs) on floats on Deadman's Pond in Gander," Pearcey says.

But even before that he was familiar with the aircraft because, as an enthusiastic young pilot, he would fly with and talk to the pilots of the different aircraft types operated by EPA every chance he got. When it came time to be officially checked out on the Beaver, he remembers no great drama. He simply absorbed what Cooper taught him about the plane, went off and practised it until it became familiar, then began piloting it on a regular basis.

"It didn't have any faults that I could detect," Pearcey said of the famous bush plane. "That's the reason it was only a matter of an hour or hour and a half (studying) and I can remember my checkout flight a couple of days later was with the chief pilot. We took off from Deadman's Pond in Gander (on June 6, 1964 flying Beaver CF-GQF) and he said we'd go out to the Ragged Harbour area, just out the coast from Gander. Now it just happened to be salmon season so he asked me if I saw that lake right there with the river running into it? He said we'd do some touch and goes there. So I did two or three and he said, 'Okay, drop me off on that rock over there and you go on (to do some more practise) and I'll keep an eye on you.' And he stood on that rock and was fishing," Pearcey remembers, laughing at the memory.

Going from the Beaver to its bigger and more sophisticated sister, the Otter, was no big thing, despite it being a significantly larger and more powerful plane. The flying characteristics, Pearcey recalls, were quite similar.

But there were still tricks of the trade to be learned. He learned, for instance, to judge when a load of freight approached the plane's weight and balance limits as it was put aboard the aircraft bobbing dockside on its floats. This was vital, because the plane could safely carry only a certain weight and, if unevenly distributed in the fuselage, could cause the plane to become unbalanced in the air, making it uncontrollable. It was a question of watching the rear portion of the floats, Pearcey explained. As the load would go aboard the floats would sink lower in the water. As long as the rear portion didn't sink beneath the surface you were pretty much within limits for weight and balance. The same operation on land was more a question of mathematics, knowing the weight of each piece of freight and loading it so it was evenly distributed inside the plane. You learned this type of stuff from talking to other pilots, as well as your own experience.

His first assignment on the Beaver was with the aircraft fitted with wheel/skis for winter flying off snow, leaving Gander in the morning with mail for northern destinations, including southern Labrador.

"From Gander we'd go in a straight line over to Harbour Deep in White Bay and then work our way up the Northern Peninsula on the eastern side, the White Bay side, and drop into various places along the way up to St. Anthony," he recalled.

St. Anthony in those days was a distribution point for the mail. EPA operated DC-3s from there and sometimes he'd be stationed there, taking the mail brought in by the DC-3s and flying it on to the small Labrador coastal communities such as Red Bay and Mary's Harbour as far north as Cartwright. It was almost impossible to do the Gander to Cartwright run and back in a day because of the distance, Pearcey remembers, but he did it a couple of times when weather was exceptionally good. In those days you could, if you weren't carrying passengers, get special permission from the tower in Gander to operate after official nightfall, something VFR-rated pilots ordinarily aren't permitted to do. In this way he built up some night flying experience, which he could legally log.

Even though he didn't have an instrument rating at this point, permitting him to legally fly in bad weather with passengers aboard, he had built up enough hours of experience to have grasped the rudiments of the art. Instrument navigation facilities in Newfoundland in the early sixties were still relatively primitive, with only an automatic direc-

tion finder (ADF) to provide guidance during flight. ADF was
an instrument on the cockpit panel with a needle that would
point to a radio navigation station that had been tuned in
ahead of time. The wind could push you off course when
following an ADF bearing, causing you to fly in a huge arc if
you weren't experienced. The system also had other limita-
tions that, to the inexperienced, could prove fatal if not
understood and compensated for. Later in the decade would
come the VOR system or **V**ery High Frequency **O**mnidirec-
tional **R**ange. It was very much better but in order to be
effective you had to be within VHF radio range to pick up the
signal it broadcast. The older ADF system at least had the
advantage of being audible over hundreds of miles.

"It was an interesting time."

And so Pearcey added the Beaver and Otter to the growing list of aircraft he was rated to fly as pilot in command. The
next step up would be a little more dramatic.

*The famous de Havilland Otter, similar to the ones Pearcey flew while working
for EPA.*

Chapter 7

Advancing

For the balance of 1964 and most of 1965 Pearcey flew the length and breadth of Newfoundland and Labrador, usually at the controls of a Beaver or an Otter with occasional returns to the Super Cubs when required by the company. But in the fall of 1965 he was introduced to a famous veteran of the Second World War, the Consolidated Catalina PBY flying boat, known to Canadians as the Canso. The province had acquired a number of the sturdy war surplus craft to serve as water bombers in the fight to protect the province's forests from the ravages of wild fires, set by careless humans or capricious nature.

Pearcey's first familiarization on the workhorse came on a November 1965 flight on a Canso bound for major overhaul work in Montreal. Up to this point all the planes on Pearcey's résumé were powered by a single engine and could be flown by a single pilot. The Canso represented more than just a doubling of complexity with its two Pratt and Whitney R-1830 "Double Wasp" 1,200 h.p. engines. It also required a co-pilot to manage the many flight systems, including the retractable undercarriage, retractable floats for water opera-

41

tion, an extendable probe for picking up water to drop on a fire, and numerous other systems. If Pearcey was to be trained as a pilot in command on these demanding beasts he'd need to upgrade his skills, including a multi-engine endorsement and an instrument flight endorsement on his pilot's license. The flight to Montreal was arranged by the company so he could receive these two important additions to his skills.

The plane on which Pearcey earned his multi-engine rating was a Cessna 310, an elegant little light twin that also saw military service with the United States Air Force as the U-3B. Instructor Joe Butrym took just three days to teach and approve Pearcey on the type. Ted recalls no great strain in rising to the challenge.

"When you were over-nighting some place, say in the winter time and everybody is stuck in, for instance, Mary's Harbour for three or four days, maybe three or four other EPA aircraft, the pilots would talk about different types of flying, aircraft, instrument ratings and all that sort of stuff."

It was an interesting and effective way to pick up piloting knowledge from more experienced pilots. And of all the places on the Labrador coast where Pearcey spent time thanks to un-cooperative weather, Mary's Harbour holds the best memories.They centre mostly on the kindness of the late Hewlett Akerman and his wife, Madelyn at whose cosy home a hot meal, a feather bed with down-filled comforter and warm welcome awaited tired pilots. A leading citizen of the town, Akerman acted as the airline's agent and provided a number of other services such as refuelling and radio-tele-phone communications.

"Very, very well liked," Pearcey said of Akerman and his wife. "They didn't want to go any place else, they wanted to spend their lives there. They loved the place and loved the people and the people loved them. So that's where we would try to stay."

Pearcey's next step up the piloting skill ladder, a more complex and demanding one, was training in instrument flying. This skill is necessary if a pilot is to fly an aircraft without visual reference to the ground or horizon, as in bad weather or at night. So, on November 9, Pearcey flew to Toronto and began his instrument flight training. Almost all of it was accomplished on a Link trainer and simulator, mechanical earthly alternatives to flying expensive airplanes around busy airports. Three weeks of hard work with little time off resulted in Pearcey being awarded his Class II instrument endorsement on November 30. By this time his log book showed about 3,000 flight hours.

Returning home, Pearcey was then checked out on another light twin, a six passenger Piper Aztec being used by EPA on the St. Pierre service. He found himself assigned this route, which would see him flying a Gander, St. Pierre, Sydney, Gander run for several months. He also did a lot of flying on the Bay d'Espoir power project, under construction at the time, reverting for the job to Beavers and Otters. But on April 13, 1966 a new chapter in Pearcey's flying career opened when he was checked out on water bomber CF-IZU by chief pilot Royal Cooper, operating out of Gander.

A week later he was assigned as co-pilot to Canso pilot Gunner Laurel to build up experience. He fought his first forest fire from the Canso's right seat on April 24, making twenty-nine drops on a fire at Bay Roberts. For a while Pearcey found himself being bounced back and forth from the water bombers to Beavers and Otters but on May 16 he began training, again under the tutelage of Cooper, as captain on the Canso. On May 19 he took off for the first time qualified as pilot in command of a water bomber with co-pilot

The Consolidated PBY Canso (also called Catalina) water bomber, similar to those flown by Pearcey in his days with EPA. This aircraft is seen in Goose Bay, Labrador in the early 1970s.

John French (who later went on to fly jets for EPA). For the balance of the 1966 forest fire season he would fly Canso CF-IGJ out of St. John's. On May 22, 1966 he did his first water drops as pilot in command on a fire in Upper Island Cove, again with French in the right seat.

The Canso was a tough bird to fly, Pearcey said, very heavy on the controls. It had no flaps, only ailerons, so slowing was done by throttle control alone. He described a water pickup:

"You would touch down on the water and keep the aircraft on the step (a skimming manoeuvre), not let it settle down in the water. You have to do that by power alone, so as soon as you touch down you start adding power, call for probe down, the co-pilot puts the probe down and by this time you've got takeoff power on and when she fills up (with water, scooped up by the probe) and the co-pilot sees this, he pulls the probe up."

The co-pilot was responsible for watching the water tanks, visible behind the cockpit in the fuselage, so he knew when they were full. As a safety feature, the plane had an overflow valve preventing the tank from being overfilled and making the plane too heavy to lift off. The pilot's primary responsibility was controlling the engine power, keeping the speeding plane on the step.

"When you've got all this power on and you're on the step and that probe comes up she wants to jump out of the water because you don't have the drag any longer of the probe sticking down," said Pearcey.

Going into lakes you'd never seen before could be touchy. You'd have to circle the lake you intended to use and check carefully for shoal areas that could rip the bottom out of the plane if struck at high speed. To do this you'd stay as high as possible because below 2,000 feet you can't usually see down through water, especially if there are waves on the surface. Both pilots would continue to eyeball the lake as altitude was lost in preparation for alighting on the water. The waves on the water and trees on the shore would reveal wind direction. You would then look for the longest run on the lake with the wind right down it and touch down as short as possible to give the maximum run while picking up water. If at any time during the pick up run the pilot became unsure if there was sufficient room left to get the plane airborne in the remaining distance, he would call for probe up and get the plane up whether the water tanks were full or not.

"It was fascinating at the time because we were all so young and full of p**s and vinegar," Pearcey said, grinning.

The danger inherent in this type of flying was not something you dwelt on, he added, looking at it rather as great fun and an high adventure.

"Most of us would have flown for nothing and to get paid for doing something that you dearly loved ... boy we wanted to fly, just go, go, go all the time."

Pearcey flew the water bombers for the balance of 1966 and, when the fire season ended, checked out in a four passenger Beech Baron light twin, again flying the St. Pierre service for the winter before returning to the water bombers in the summer of 1967.

As it turned out, 1967 was the last summer Pearcey would spend as a full time water bomber pilot. That summer also marked a personal low point with the loss of two close friends in separate crashes.

By the spring of 1967 Ted was a check/training pilot for EPA, training and checking out pilots on various types of aircraft in the fleet. One such was Neil Bridger, a young pilot he checked out in a Canadian-designed bush plane called the Found FBA-2C (on floats) that EPA used in Churchill Falls for a year or so on an experimental basis. Pearcey didn't like the plane much, finding it heavy on the controls and underpowered with its Avco-Lycoming flat six engine. Bridger, like many young pilots, had gotten his basic pilot ratings and joined EPA as a co-pilot on water bombers but wanted to become a pilot in command. To achieve that desire he needed to be trained on the smaller, single engine planes in the fleet first which he could fly by himself. Bridger had very few hours built up at this time but Pearcey brought him to the point where he believed he had sufficient training to handle the Found safely. Pearcey then went to Labrador on the water bombers for a busy 1967 fire season. Later that summer Bridger was sent to Williamsport in White Bay with the

Found, carrying four Japanese businessmen who were interested in buying an old whaling station there.

"They told me afterwards that he was briefed on this place where he was landing," Pearcey recalled. "Usually the wind there was coming down over a hill where you landed from the bay into the harbour and if there was any substantial wind you don't go in there because you could get a downdraught just as you were trying to land (or take off). Anyway, he was briefed on making sure when he took off to go way out the harbour in the event that when he got off the water she wouldn't climb because of downdraughts off the hill ahead ... obviously he miscalculated, took off and just got out of the water with the hill directly ahead of him and he's not half way up the hill yet ... so he makes a screaming left hand turn, stalls out in the turn and kills everybody on board. The aircraft came to rest right on the beach where the plant was."

Pearcey felt, and still feels, that if Bridger had had more training he would have approached the situation differently and was partly a victim of his low airtime. He also felt the plane bore a substantial part of the blame because it didn't have the power or manoeuvrability to get itself out of a situation that could have been handled easily by a Beaver or even a Cessna 185. Found Brothers Aviation went out of business in 1968 after building and selling less than forty planes.

Worse was to follow.

Ron Penny and Ted Pearcey were buddies in the best sense of the word. They shared an apartment together, went on holidays together, were the best of friends. Before leaving Newfoundland for Labrador that summer of 1967, Pearcey had been training Penny as pilot in command of the Canso. Before leaving for Labrador he met the chief pilot, who asked him how Penny was coming with his training.

"And I said, he's my best friend and I don't know how he's going to take this, he's going to be pretty mad, I assume, but I think he needs a lot more training, especially in (handling) porpoising."

Porpoising is a sort of bounding motion that develops when a plane is not touched down on water in the correct attitude. In a Canso it can be deadly because if you don't control it immediately it becomes more severe with each impact until the plane will nose straight down into the water.

"And that's exactly what happened. [Penny was sent] to the Stephenville area and when he (arrived) there was a dead calm and no lakes around to pick up water so he used the ocean. Dead calm, but no matter how dead calm the ocean is, there's always a swell, even though there might not be a ripple on the water. And here he was with the worst type of conditions to produce porpoising and obviously he decided to pick up (water), it was the only place he could pick up. The people who saw it said the aircraft touched down and it bounced up and went down — went up again and down again — [and on the third bounce], dug in nose first."

Both pilots were killed instantly.

Pearcey came as close that day as he ever did in his career to quitting flying when he got the news of his friend's death. As it turned out, he never again flew water bombers regularly. A week after Penny's death he was on a commercial plane to Toronto to pick up a brand new de Havilland Twin Otter.

Chapter 8

Maturing

*O*n July 14, 1967 Ted Pearcey was introduced to the Twin Otter, a plane many aviators feel is perhaps the closest thing yet devised to the legendary DC-3 as the universal workhorse of the air. Designed and built by de Havilland Aircraft of Downsview, Ontario, 844 of the trusty twin turboprop planes would be built in a two-decade span, and some estimates have over 700 of them still airworthy today. Pearcey's introduction to the plane was compliments of de Havilland's chief engineering test pilot at the time, Bob Fowler.

Although equipped with floats, the plane that day sat high and dry on beaching gear, on a seaplane ramp at Toronto Island Airport in Lake Ontario. Emblazoned on the vertical tail was the registration CF-DMR, the last three letters chosen by Pearcey to represent Department of Mines and Resources, as the government department operating the aircraft was then known. Pearcey already had flight experience on the Twin Otter in its land configuration of tricycle landing gear, having taken a familiarization course in June. But this would be his first flight in a float-equipped version. The original Twin Otter prototype aircraft, CF-DHC-X, had been mounted on floats successfully in 1966 but Pearcey believes DMR was the first production aircraft sold in the float configuration.

"It was the most beautiful thing," Pearcey recalls, his expression revealing his clear memories of the occasion.

"It had such capabilities. You could jump into the air in a matter of yards. The (cruising) speed was pretty good at about 140 knots, which wasn't too bad on floats. You could land it on water and the passengers wouldn't know it was on the water. There was nothing like it."

He remembers that first flight well, impressed by the craft's shear size and sleek good looks. He was especially impressed that it was possible to start both engines, let go the lines holding it to the dock and hold it in place by putting the propellers in neutral pitch (angling the blades to change the direction of the thrust they provide) and then manoeuvre the plane on the water by increasing the pitch for forward motion, reversing it to back up or using different pitch on each prop to turn. Asked to compare it to the single engine Otter or other twin engined planes he'd flown, Pearcey found himself unable to do so, "because the Twin Otter was *so* much easier to handle, it had so much capability."

It was a nice plane to fly, said Pearcey, with auto pilot and radar. And it flew just fine on one engine, as he found out one night on a flight from Deer Lake to St. John's. One engine began to "surge," unable to maintain a steady flow of power, and the instrument panel gauges were indicating that all was not well. Radioing company headquarters in St. John's for advice, Pearcey was told to shut down the ailing powerplant if he felt it necessary and land at Gander, which was close by at the time. Single engine flight is a required part of every pilot's training when upgrading his license to qualify for operation of aircraft with more than one powerplant and

Pearcey had been trained in the necessary techniques on a number of aircraft, including the Twin Otter.

"So, we just shut her down and turned left and went into Gander, just like normal once you have it trimmed out (adjusted to compensate for the lost power). The speed hardly dropped off at all," Pearcey recalled.

Pearcey had already gained experience with the Pratt & Whitney PT-6A turbine engines that powered the plane from having previously flown the single engine turbo Beaver, powered by the same engine, so that made the transition to the larger, more complex twin easier. His check out on the plane by Fowler in Toronto took less than 3½ hours of flying time over two days. Then came a brief waiting period while final cosmetic touches were made to the plane. But on July 29 Pearcey and EPA engineer Clint Shannon were airborne for Newfoundland, with a fuel stop in Sept Isle, Quebec, touching down in Gander after a total flying time of seven hours and thirty-five minutes. Pearcey flew home to St. John's later that evening but was back in Gander on the 31st to fly the new plane to Goose Bay, St. Anthony and back to Gander in four hours and forty minutes. Later that day he took up EPA chief pilot Royal Cooper on a checkout flight for about an hour. Next day he checked out pilot Marsh Jones on the plane and the day after that Palmer Tibbo. After that it was regular government flying, carrying such people as premier Joey Smallwood, Ed Roberts, O.L. Vardy, former broadcaster-turned-politician John Nolan and his wife, Andrew Crosbie and family, John Crosbie, and other prominent government and business people of the day. Home "field" for the plane was Octagon Pond while a new base was being built on Paddy's Pond. The Twin Otter, Pearcey remembered, caused a stir everywhere he went, especially among other pilots.

"They all wanted to get a board and get a ride. I sneaked a couple of rides for guys. I had something 'didn't seem right' " he said with a wink, "and said I needed to do a short test flight, and I'd take two or three of the guys."

Several flights in the Twin Otter stand out in Pearcey's memory. For instance, there was the first time he landed on "the button" of runway 29 in St. John's. The button is a concrete pad at each end of the runway where heavily loaded planes will do their engine runups, checking that all systems are operating normally, before committing to takeoff. It is 300 feet long and is not intended to be landed on. Ordinarily, a plane coming in for a landing will pass low over the button before touching down on the main asphalt section of the runway. But one day, just to prove he could do it, Pearcey came in and landed right on the button.

"I landed as short as I could on the button at 40 knots, hanging on the props and, as soon as she touched down, applied full reverse thrust on the props and she stopped in about 150 feet, half the distance of the button," said Pearcey, grinning like a kid who knows he's been caught doing something naughty, but proud of himself anyway.

After that first time he'd demonstrate the technique to people if they asked, and the conditions for doing so were safe. The little trick was eventually reported to Joey Smallwood who, on a flight one day, requested a demonstration. Pearcey complied and Joey was delighted. He also got Pearcey to demonstrate the airplane's capability to fly safely on one engine, something Joey delighted in doing when he had other passengers aboard the plane. An enthusiastic flyer, the premier also enjoyed encouraging Pearcey to do the smoothest possible water landings, pointing out to passengers that the transition from flying to landing was so smooth that, with eyes closed, it was almost impossible to tell when the plane was actually on the water and no longer flying.

"He used to get a big kick out of it. Joey Smallwood was the best person that I ever worked for or with. As a matter of fact, a government minister got p****d off one time when we were trying to take off in a Beaver, going to Twillingate. I got out on the pond and Joey was up in the cockpit in the right hand seat and I had a mag drop.* So I tried it a couple of times,

T. Pearcey collection

Ted Pearcey (right) with Premier Joseph Smallwood aboard the sealing ship Chesley A. Crosbie *just before the collapse of the seal fishery.*

---

* electrical impulses to the ignition system that, if below a given level, reduce the power output of the engine.

got her up on the step but no way would she fly so I had to bring her into the dock again."

The minister proceeded to curse Pearcey out for not having checked the plane out earlier but Joey quickly jumped to his defense.

"Joey turned around and says, 'What do you know about airplanes?' When the offending minister could only stutter out a word or two, Joey promptly told him to shut up. He says, 'do you think the captain is doing this on purpose?' Then he looked at me and winked."

Joey would often come up and sit in the right seat when he felt the urge, but he wasn't interested in taking the controls. He left that to Pearcey, whom he invariably called Captain. On only a few occasions can Pearcey ever recall Joey calling him Ted.

Pearcey retains a guest book which he bought and carried aboard the Twin Otter when it first went into service. The very first signature is Joey's, dated August 1967. On following lines can be seen such names as (then) Lt. Governor Fabian O'Dea, Pierre Trudeau, Viscount Bernard Montgomery of Alamein, (then) Governor General Roland Michener, broadcasters Freeman White of CJCN radio and Elmer Harris of CKCM radio in Grand Falls, Charles Taylor (then Chancellor of Memorial University) and many others. One of the people to leave the biggest impression on Pearcey was Pierre Trudeau, who visited the province in the summer of 1968 before going into an election that fall which he won to become Prime Minister. Convinced that Trudeau was destined for victory, Joey got him to come to the province to show him around and, no doubt, pave the way to a smooth relationship when he took the reins of federal power.

"We went into a number of places (in the Twin Otter), we were gone the whole day. On our way back to Gander Joey came up and says, 'Captain, do you know that the Prime Minister — and I'm not being forward because he *is* going to be the Prime Minister, is a pilot?' And I said, 'Oh really sir, I didn't know that.'

"So he said, 'Well not really a pilot but he's taken some flying lessons. Would you mind if he came up?' I said not at all sir, and up comes Trudeau, puts his seat belt on without being told (which impressed Pearcey). "I said, 'according to the premier sir, you've done some flying?' 'No, not much,' he replied and I said, 'Would you like to take over?' He said, 'oh, all right' so I flipped off the autopilot and he tried it."

It may have been a bit uncomfortable for those in the back. Trudeau promptly began to climb and dive, bank and turn and Pearcey remembers all conversation from the back of the plane ceasing. After a short while Joey came back up front and asked Trudeau how he liked the plane, to which Trudeau replied he liked it fine. Then he asked Pearcey what he thought of Trudeau as a pilot. Summoning his best diplomacy, Pearcey replied: "Well sir, let me put it this way. If he's not successful in October, I'll offer him a job as my co-pilot." And Joey, who was crouching down between the pilot and co-pilot seats, laughed so hard he slapped his hands on the floor. "Did you hear that sir, did you hear that?" he said to Trudeau. Trudeau just sat there with a big grin on his face but Joey, Pearcey said, "broke right up."

In another encounter with Trudeau, about a year later, Pearcey was impressed when the Prime Minister recognized him on a flight to Churchill Falls and came over to shake his hand and chat for a minute.

"I thought that was fantastic."

Another impressive guest he had aboard DMR was Field Marshall Bernard Law Montgomery of Alamein, one of the most famous of Allied World War Two generals and the commanding officer of many Newfoundlanders enlisted in the British Army. It was on May 19, 1968 and Pearcey was given the job of flying the Twin Otter to Gander where he was to meet Monty's overseas flight and fly him on to Octagon Pond in St. John's. There was a terrific scene there, Pearcey clearly recalls, Topsail Road and the shores of the pond choked with people and cars. After shutting down the engines and having the plane secured to the dock, Pearcey got out and stood at the bottom of the steps to see Monty and his entourage out.

"Out he comes. He ducks under the door and stands up. Then I made an awful boo boo. He started down the steps and I just put out my hand to maybe help him. Well, he looked at me and I just about froze and I put my hand down again ... what a look he gave me. I learned a lot about protocol that day."

Nevertheless, he was one of Pearcey's most admired passengers and he proudly displays his signature in the guest book, Montgomery of Alamein, F.M. (Field Marshall), in a firm, flowing script.

"Isn't that something to have? I'm glad I put this (book) in the airplane when I did."

Pearcey flew DMR regularly for two years and now looks back fondly on the time. DMR, unfortunately, had a short career in Newfoundland and Labrador. It was sold in 1973 to a company in the North West Territories and was later damaged in a crash. Repaired, it flew on until eventually retired due to old age.

But change was in the air for Pearcey's career, which was about to take an entirely new path. The change first made itself known in the person of William Callahan, then a minister in the Smallwood cabinet.

Chapter 9

Government Service

For some time the provincial government had been considering the economies of setting up its own air service as opposed to the existing practice of buying aircraft and having them maintained and flown by a third party. Pearcey recalls a day when he was flying Joey Smallwood in the Twin Otter and, there being no other passengers aboard, he asked Pearcey to come back into the cabin for a private chat. Not knowing quite what to expect, Pearcey turned the controls over to his copilot and went back to the passenger cabin.

"And he said, 'what do other provinces do that maybe we should be doing in the way of aviation? Which provinces have their own air division?' Obviously someone had been talking to him," Pearcey recalled. He replied that the provinces he knew for sure were operating their own air service divisions at that time were Quebec, Ontario, Alberta and B.C., with B.C. then being the acknowledged leader in air ambulance service.

"I don't know how it all came about," Pearcey says now, but insists he was not involved in any decision-making process. He recalls being called up one day a short time later by Bill

Callahan, then the minister of Mines and Resources, and asked what he was doing next day. Pearcey indicated he had the day clear.

Callahan came and picked him up in a car next morning and off they went to Joey's home on Roache's Line. As Pearcey remembers it, the Premier did all the talking, explaining that they were aware of other province's air operations. There was also the perception at that time that EPA was attempting to get away from operating the smaller airplanes in its fleet to concentrate more on scheduled service with larger passenger aircraft including, eventually, jets. This was around the time EPA had landed millions in government money needed to buy modern turbo prop airliners.

"The whole thing just seemed to evolve without any fuss or meetings or anything like that," Pearcey recalled. "I was never to a meeting except (that day at Joey's house.)"

"Mrs. Smallwood served us lunch."

Bill Callahan, now semi-retired and living in St. John's, was privy to many of the details which were not available to Pearcey at the time. In July of 1968 he became the minister of Mines and Resources, as the department was then called, in the Smallwood Liberal cabinet, and EPA was then the chief provider of aero services to government on a lease arrangement, with the exception of helicopter services which were being supplied by other companies. As Callahan recalls, government was then operating a dozen or more aircraft which it had bought, turned over to EPA and which it then leased back from the company complete with crews, maintenance and repair as required. After about a year as minister Callahan felt a better deal could be obtained by government if it put its aviation requirements out to tender among the several companies then sniffing around for business, including Atlantic Aviation of Montreal, a subsidiary of Atlantic Aviation

Corporation of Wilmington, Delaware. The idea was to have the successful bidder come in and operate the service for a couple of years, training Newfoundlanders in all the necessary skills to be able to take over the entire operation at the end of the contract, the resulting organization to then be operated as a department of government. But if government could have persuaded EPA to accept that deal, they would have, Callahan recalled.

"In meetings with these guys (EPA management) I simply told them that we wanted a better deal and if they couldn't provide us with what we felt was equitable then under the circumstances, we'd have to go to tender."

Meetings continued for months but EPA could not be persuaded to meet government's requirements, so a tender call was made with Atlantic Aviation eventually being chosen the winner from three companies which submitted bids. With EPA now being phased out of the business, government began to set up a headquarters in St. John's on property on the east side of the airport then, as now, known as hanger 3. By the time Pearcey was eventually invited to Roache's Line to be offered the position of Director of Government Air Services and chief pilot, many of the above mentioned decisions had already been made by cabinet and Pearcey may have been a little taken aback by the offer from Joey. But he took little convincing to accept the position.

At the same time he made it plain the job was too big for just one man and that he'd need a team with experts in the various functions such as engineering, records keeping, stores, financial control, office support, and all the other myriad specialties needed to efficiently and safely run what amounted to a small air force. All of this was eventually to be supplied by Atlantic Aviation so Joey agreed and the deal was struck.

"I made no difference to the government reaching this decision, because it was (already) done," Pearcey said of his installation in the job

Callahan feels, to this day, that the decision to hire Pearcey for the position was the right one and that Joey Smallwood concurred.

"My recollection is that there was no resistance or hesitation (from Joey). He sort of looked at (the plan) and said 'why haven't we done this before? Why have we waited all this time? ... and since we know Pearcey is a proven professional I don't know why we haven't hired him long ago.' To go over there and make the deal that day, I'm not sure Ted had anticipated that."

Right away Pearcey saw the job as a challenge. He left EPA with no hard feelings, seeing the government's offer rather as a chance to take on a new, interesting job coupled with the benefits and security offered by a civil service position, something not many pilots get to enjoy.

Once the decision was made and Atlantic Aviation began to form an effective team, the company proceeded to bring in all the necessary personnel to set up and supervise training. It was made clear to them that, wherever possible, they were to hire the people that would be displaced from EPA as government took over the operations, which was accomplished on a gradual transition basis. Pearcey was government's man in all this but left much of the daily operations to Atlantic while he flew, spending as much time as necessary coordinating with Atlantic's management team.

One part of job Pearcey hated was having to turn down people who applied for jobs, or make decisions about the careers of fellow fliers in his role as check pilot. A lot of the pilots were his personal friends, some like brothers. But he felt it necessary in the name of safety to be, in his own words, "a nit picker," a feeling only reinforced by the earlier deaths of his friends and colleagues Neil Bridger and Ron Penny in 1967. He would always be burdened with the feeling they may have lived had he been pickier in their cases. This deliberate attitude, he knew, could and would draw criticism but he remains convinced to this day it that it would have been an abrogation of both his knowledge and responsibility to demand less than the best from any pilot flying under his control.

"I wasn't picky enough in two cases," Pearcey lamented. "To have to tell a guy (who was trying to upgrade to a more complex aircraft type) that he better stay where he is because this thing wasn't for him, that's tough. I didn't like that."

A point of friction for Pearcey in the beginning was the deputy minister he found himself reporting to, a man he felt resented having Pearcey and this new-fangled air services attached to his department, airplanes being a topic completely outside his knowledge.

"I guess somebody told him that he didn't have to know anything about aircraft, we'll just put the air division under this department and the director of the air division (Pearcey) will report and confer and everything else with the deputy minister or the assistant deputy minister," Pearcey noted.

But he still felt he was resented and that the man just didn't want to know anything about it. He also felt some other people resented his position because Ed Roberts, who he described as "quite a pusher" of the air service, served as a conduit for Pearcey to the premier's office. Roberts knew enough about aviation to understand what Pearcey was trying to do. Pearcey felt he had a good rapport with Roberts.

"Ed Roberts was the man that I was *unofficially* told to keep in contact with and I guess the deputy minister of the department that the aircraft was assigned to resented this fact and word got around: 'who does this guy Pearcey think he is?' So I had a very bad setup facing me."

But gradually, perhaps because two diverse personalities began to reach a little understanding of each other, things changed for the better and the situation eventually resolved itself. As a result, Pearcey has fond memories of just about everybody he worked with during his government years, especially the pilots.

"All the guys were good. Now, they all had different personalities ... but they've all done well."

In 1973 government decided to invest in a Beech King Air for air ambulance and executive work. They'd sold the Twin Otter on May 1st of that year and began leasing a Beech B90 King Air on a temporary basis. When the decision was made to buy, they settled on the later model King Air A100 which they ordered brand new from the factory in Whicita, Kansas.

Pearcey (centre) takes delivery of Beech King Air A100, registered CF-GNL in Whichita, Kansas in November of 1973. The men flanking him are Beech employees. This aircraft today is fitted out as an air ambulance and continues to fly "medivacs" around the province.

Pearcey was mightily impressed with the King Air.

"I was flying trucks before ... it was just a different atmosphere all together," he said, but adding quickly that every pilot feels that way when upgrading to a more sophisticated type of aircraft than he's flown in the past.

But there was no denying the Beech was a lot faster than the Twin Otter, could fly much higher and thus stay above the weather thanks to the pressurized cabin.

Chapter 10

Parting of the Ways with Government

The first PC government since Confederation took office in June 1972. Now in opposition, it became the Liberal's job to screw the PCs any way they could. Pearcey learned that right away.

Two of the people he soon came into conflict with were Liberal MHAs Steve Neary and Tom Lush who were making accusations about government members using government aircraft for their own pleasure, as opposed to legitimate government business.

Some of that may have gone on, Pearcey acknowledges, but it had under the Liberals too. New premier Frank Moores, like Smallwood before him, was an enthusiastic flyer, but more for the convenience of it than the sensation of being airborne.

In early 1978 Pearcey made a mistake that would eventually lead to another career shift. He took a one week holiday, to which he was entitled, and used it to fly to Texas to pick up a helicopter for Craig Dobbin, a friend since the 1950s. Dobbin had recently formed Sealand Helicopters and was competing for government business with Universal, who had long had a virtual monopoly because they were the only helicopter company of any size operating in the province. By this time government's air fleet consisted pretty much of just the King Air and the water bombers with other air work being contracted out to helicopters. Neary and Lush, Pearcey contends, saw in his perfectly innocent and legitimate offer to help out a friend a conflict of interest and went after Pearcey in the House of Assembly. There was eventually a Public Accounts Committee hearing into the whole mess and in June 1978, Pearcey decided it was time to wash his hands of the whole business and resign. The accusation, much to Pearcey's disgust, was also made that he was carrying a small portable tape recorder with him whenever he piloted a government plane and taping the conversations of government passengers. In fact, what had been called a tape recorder was actually a pager so that he could be reached when an emergency medivac flight was needed.

A front page story in the June 13, 1978 *Daily News* quoted Pearcey describing a number of PC members as scum, hypocrites and worse and professing himself as "bitter and ... fed up" and "glad to be out of the whole mess."

T. Pearcey collection

Pearcey poses with a Bell 206 Jet Ranger purchased by Craig Dobbin. As a favour to his friend, Pearcey took a week's holiday and flew to Texas to pick up the aircraft and ferry it back to St. John's. Little did he know the consequences of this seemingly simple act.

Chapter 11

Whirlybirds

Ted Pearcey's love affair with helicopters began in 1975 while he was still working for government when his friend, businessman Noel Hutton (who'd had a succession of small float planes) decided he wanted a chopper to make getting to his favourite fishing spots easier. Pearcey had flown *in* choppers as part of his work for Government Services, and liked it a lot, but he had never piloted one. He got a call from Hutton one day announcing he was going to Ontario to look at buying a used helicopter and wanted Pearcey to go along with him. They went and in short order Hutton had made the deal, purchasing a Bell Jet Ranger. The dealer checked out both Hutton and Pearcey on the craft, a task that took about three days, to the point where they both were awarded their private rotary wing license. The two then flew the whirlybird back to Newfoundland and thereafter Pearcey flew it quite often, building up several hundred hours of experience.

In 1979, after leaving government, he took about two weeks in Texas to get a commercial helicopter ticket. In the meantime Hutton had bought a brand new 206B, C-FMNR,

T. Pearcey collection

The Cessna Citation business jet on which Pearcey got his multi-engined jet training. circa 1978.

(later sold to a fish processing company) to replace the used one he'd bought a few years before.

Having now left government services, Pearcey took a contract job with a Sydney, N.S. fish processing company that had three helicopters. But he was hired primarily to oversee the fitting out of a Cessna Citation business jet the company had on order, deliver it and hire its crew. In this way Pearcey got checked out on twin engine jets. Pearcey and the two pilots he'd hired attended both ground and flight school on the craft and it was soon delivered to the company. This contract kept him busy for a couple of months.

Next came a brief contract job with Field Aviation of Toronto, the Beechcraft retailer, to do some demonstration flights in the Maritimes of a new Beech Duchess 76, a four-place, T-tail light twin. This was a short job, only lasting about

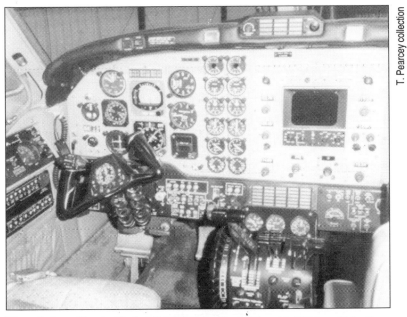

The cockpit, or "front office" of C-FPCD, the Beech King Air 200 bought by the newly named Atlantic Airways in 1983.

two weeks but he immediately picked up another contract which lasted into February of the next year, 1979. It was with Dennison Mines, flying their Beech King Air 200. He also took the company owner's son, Stephen Roman, who was working on his private license, on as copilot to help him with his instruction. Most of this time was spent flying in and out of the mine site at Elliott Lake to places like Goderich, Sudbury and Toronto. The opportunity could have become a full time position but Pearcey found he didn't like the job that much and decided to look elsewhere.

Again, he found himself looking for something to fly. In July he signed a contract with Mobil Oil which had leased a King Air 200 from the United States. But it was undergoing major scheduled maintenance. While waiting for that to be completed he got a call from Bert Patcy of Labrador Airways

in Happy Valley-Goose Bay to pick up and deliver a new
Beech 88 Queen Air the company had just bought. This job
was quickly completed and on July 10 Pearcey was in St.
John's to start the contract for Mobil.

This was to be an intense period of flying. Many of the
flights were of ten-plus hours, taking drill crew members
back and forth from Frobisher Bay to St. John's and points in
between. They would leave St. John's at 6 a.m., go direct to
Frobisher Bay, arrive around noon local time and go to bed.
An established northern airline, First Air, would then take the
crews on to their final destination where the dirt runway was
too short for the King Air, then bring a crew back to Frobisher
for the return ride to St. John's, where they'd arrive around
midnight. It was a punishing schedule, but fortunately limited, and it ended without incident on September 26, 1979.

Chapter 12

Into Business

Returning to St. John's, Pearcey found more than just work. He was about to enter the business world. It happened when he hooked up with local businessmen Tom Collingwood and Robert Snow. Collingwood had recently bought out a flying school/charter operation owned by Eli Squires and saw the opportunity to expand. He was, as Pearcey put it, the money man, Pearcey was to be the flyer and Snow the organizer. Thus did he become an equal partner of a newly minted company they called Aztec Aviation.

The operation prospered despite the early, tragic loss of Snow who became ill not long after they got the business up and running, dying a short time later. Pearcey and Collingwood bought out his share of the company from his estate and became co-owners.

The fleet of the new company included a Piper Aztec light twin and several Piper Cherokees which were employed as trainers for the flying school. Pearcey wasn't interested in the flying school. It was Snow's baby and after he died they hired an employee to run it. Meanwhile, the decision was made to get into slightly larger planes, twin engine craft capable of instrument flying in all kinds of weather and doing passenger charters to St. Pierre & Miquelon. They soon bought a Piper Navajo which was later replaced by a larger & more powerful Piper Chieftain. Then they landed a contract to patrol the transatlantic cable that carried phone lines to Europe. The cable would sometimes get hooked by draggers fishing on the continental shelf, damaging it. Their job was to spot fishing boats in area, drop leaflets (in several languages) warning them of the cable below them on the ocean bed and note their position and identity in case a problem developed that could be traced back to them at that time and place. Pearcey recalls three or four occasions when the cable was damaged or broken. A special cable ship would have to be sent out to the site of the damage to raise it to surface and repair it.

This job, which didn't require flying every day but only when told to by the cable company, was accomplished with the same plane they were using for the St. Pierre-Miquelon charters. The over water navigation, by today's standards, was a bit primitive, using a system called Omega, later replaced by LORAN. But they often found themselves, of necessity, using dead reckoning.* Pearcey didn't mind the offshore work. He wasn't keeping detailed logs at the time but figures the contract lasted a couple of years.

In the meantime they were also using the plane for such jobs as medivacs and business charters, minimizing money-losing down time. Aztec Aviation prospered.

---

* Originally ded (for deduced) reckoning, estimating your position based on your compass heading, air speed, and allowing for drift caused by wind.

By 1983 the decision was made to go after bigger contracts, doing ice patrols for the offshore oil companies that were exploring the Grand Banks with drill rigs of various types and sizes. Around this time, local businessman Craig Dobbin was involved in talks with Collingwood.

Early that year they began looking for a better plane, eventually finding a Beech King Air 200 in the U.S. which they bought and registered C-FPCD for, Pearcey, Collingwood and Dobbin, and changed the company name to Atlantic Airways. This same plane today flies regularly from St. John's on ice and fishery patrols on a charter contract. But the advent of the new company with its bigger planes and bigger plans was to be the prelude to Pearcey's departure. To this day he is circumspect about the details but feels it all started around this time when a decision was made to ease him out of the company if possible. Collingwood, he said, asked Pearcey to stop or severely cut back his cockpit time and spend more time flying a desk for the company in a management position. Pearcey resisted. Matters came to a head shortly after Collingwood, Pearcey and their families returned from a vacation in Florida. After some wrangling among lawyers for both sides, Pearcey was bought out of the partnership. But the financial settlement he reached at least gave him some breathing room until he found another flying job.

Chapter 13

Rotary Days

While still involved with Atlantic Airways, Pearcey had built up about 300 hours in helicopters, mostly on his friend Noel Hutton's Bell Jet Ranger. He'd delivered a Jet Ranger for a St. John's business in 1980 and did some flying for them, as well as for several other companies who'd invested in rotary wing aircraft..

So it seemed only logical to set up a company, which he called Executive Helicopters Ltd., to operate these aircraft on a contractual basis. He made sure he always had another pilot he could call on if his regular job kept him from making a flight when asked, but did as much of the flying as possible himself, going where and when the company personnel wanted.

For this service he was paid a basic monthly rate plus an hourly flying rate. After leaving Atlantic Airways in 1983 it seemed only logical to concentrate on Executive Helicopters, which he did until he retired.

He was particularly fond of the helicopter's relative immunity to wind when landing and taking off. Float planes, in particular, are susceptible to wind problems when approach-

T. Pearcey collection

One of the Bell 206 Jet Rangers Pearcey flew during the days of Executive Helicopters. The craft is seen on the Gander River.

ing or leaving a dock and can be a handful for the most experience pilot. A fixed wing aircraft must be in motion in order to counteract the wind's influence on landing or takeoff but a helicopter, with its ability to hover, can be reduced to zero forward speed and turned in its own length into the wind, no matter what direction it is blowing from.

"That way, it's fantastic. What a difference," Pearcey enthuses.

Ted Pearcey made his last commercial flight on Aug. 3, 1995 when he ferried Bell Jet Ranger C-FMNR from Goose Bay to St. John's. He flew privately a bit after that but not much.

Today, from the vantage point of a new century and with over 15,000 hours in his fixed wing and helicopter log books, Pearcey looks back and admits to some regrets, chief of which was the time his profession kept him away from his family. But he loved flying.

"The thing is, if you had the feeling that I had towards flying, you'd end up flying for somebody and if they didn't want to pay you you'd fly for them anyway," he says with a rueful chuckle.

He regrets that he could have made more if he'd sold himself a little more dearly. He sees now that some of the people he flew for, who he thought of as friends, were first and foremost employers, to whom the holy grail of money was always the bottom line.

"If they can get you, like in my case where they knew I would probably fly their aircraft for them for nothing, they sort of had me by the ... well, you know. I feel very stupid. I gave myself away for nothing."

Yes, he did manage a living wage but looking back on it now Pearcey feels if he'd gone more into the business end of flying, perhaps he'd be better off today.

"I really wouldn't presume to talk any young person into getting into aviation. I wouldn't even presume to tell them how great flying is. Kids love that, but I've gone through it and I know that you're not going to make a lot of money."

In addition to the time away from home, there's also the stress of passing twice yearly physicals and twice yearly check rides, the failure of any of which can bring a career to a screeching halt.

"That's four times a year you had to face (the possibility of) losing your income and no other profession has to do that," he points out.

Pearcey wouldn't encourage or discourage his grandchildren when it comes to flying. His son, now an accomplished pilot with Canadian Helicopters, was, as a child, the one who never wanted to go flying with Dad. But his daughter, the journalist, would sit in the co-pilot seat and take the controls. It's a contradiction not lost on Pearcey.

"So how can you tell how people are going to decide on a future and what will influence them in their choice?"

Chapter 14

A Case of Salvage: One More Story

Back in the days of flying the Twin Otter for EPA, Pearcey remembers getting a call from the premier's office to fly the incumbent Lieutenant Governor and his party to a fishing lodge on the Serpentine River on the west coast, near Port au Port. The trip was a routine one and accomplished without difficulty. A week later he was to go back and pick the party up. That proved considerably less than routine.

With co-pilot Robert March in the right seat they set out from St. John's for the west coast on a beautiful day until arriving over Bay St. George. A low fog bank lay offshore. As they parallelled the coastline on the way to the mouth of the Serpentine, the fog was closing in on them like a pincer, leaving them an ever-narrowing corridor of clear air. Still, they reached their destination and were prepared for a quick pickup and turnaround that would have gotten them safely airborne before the fog closed in — if the party had been there. They weren't.

That meant circling the area in the hope their engine noise would let the group know they were there and hurry them up a bit. Finally, a boat was seen coming out the mouth of the river so they landed immediately. The fog was almost upon them as they taxied in toward the shore.

"All of a sudden we realized that the fog was following us faster than we were taxiing. We were getting pretty close in and we couldn't go any further because of the rocks and shoals. So I just turned around and started out and was going to take off again," Pearcey recalls.

It wasn't to be. In order to take off they'd have to fly right into the fog. Before they knew what was happening the fog had closed in completely. Pearcey was forced to stop his engines for fear of running into something, perhaps a fishing boat. Every once in a while the fog would lift a tiny bit and they'd begin to taxi in hope of breaking out of the fog into a clear patch , and back into the sky.

"So we just kept taxiing and we finally got to a place where you could see maybe a hundred feet, so I paralleled the shoreline and we taxied some more but conditions got worse and worse. But finally we saw a boat so we cut the power right away and the boat saw us and came over ... and the skipper said 'where are you going?'

"And I said 'I don't think we're going any place.'"

As luck would have it, the fishing boat was headed into nearby Lark Harbour so Pearcey asked if he could follow them in.

"'You can, but what happens if you lose sight of us?' the boat owner asked. 'I'll put a line on you.' So we tied a line to each float and he started towing us."

The boat was only thirty feet away but the fog had gotten so thick Pearcey and March often could hardly see it from their seats in the cockpit. Finally the boat slowed and the skipper called out that they were nearly there. Pearcey wanted him to let go the ropes at this point, firing up the engines and staying very close behind the boat as it made its way into the harbour. But the skipper was very reluctant, insisting he would tow them right in.

Pearcey had realized that if they were towed right into the harbour the boat captain and crew might be able to lodge a salvage claim against the plane, valued at somewhere in the vicinity of a half million dollars. Saying he'd see the skipper inside and "take care of him" for his trouble, Pearcey cast off the lines and they taxied safely into the harbour under their own power. Once the Otter was tied securely to a buoy, the Skipper offered to get them a meal or a place to stay.

"This guy wanted to get us off the airplane so badly," Pearcey remembers, chuckling.

They were soon able to get a drum of fuel to top up their tanks and when the weather cleared next day they were able to take off, landing without further incident in Corner Brook. The vice regal party was retrieved later by four wheel drive vehicle and returned safely home.

"About a week later the phone rings (and premier Smallwood says) 'Captain, can you come up and see me?' So I went up to his office and he says 'what happened to you and the Lieutenant Governor?' But before I could answer he said, 'I've got a fellow who came in and saw me this morning and he wants me to pay him $5,000 for saving the Twin Otter.'"

Pearcey explained the situation in detail but said the man certainly deserved something because if he hadn't come along when he did the situation could have gotten much worse. Discussions with the Justice Department indicated the man might indeed have a case should he decide to pursue it in court and perhaps the best thing to do was offer him a settlement.

"So Joey says, 'All right, we'll take care of that but you're not going to do that again, are you?' with a big grin on his face. He really liked me you know, and I felt it. And I had a lot of time for him too."

The media never got wind of the story.

Appendix I

LIST OF AIRCRAFT PEARCEY FLEW

Individual types flown: Aeronca Champ; Aero Commander 680FP and 690 Turbo; Sea Bee; Bell Jet Ranger (helicopter); Beech 234, Baron, Duchess, Queen Air B80, King Air 90, 100 and 200; Cessna 170, 172, 180, 182, 310, 421 and Cessna Citation (jet); Consolidated PBY-5A Canso; de Havilland Beaver, Turbo Beaver, Otter, Twin Otter and DH 125 (jet); Travel Air; Found FBA-2c; IAI Westwind (jet); Lear 25 (jet); Merlin 2b and IV; Piper Super Cub, Seneca, Aztec and Navaho; , over 30 types.

Pearcey's Qualifications: single engine, land and sea and amphibian: twin engine, land and sea and amphibian: single engine turbo prop, land and sea : multi engine turbo prop, land and sea: multi-engine jet: helicopter (Bell 206): instrument flight rating (IFR): night rating: multi-engine endorsement: float endorsement.

Appendix II

SOURCES:

The majority of the information presented in this book has been gathered from many hours of personal interviews with Ted Pearcey in which he drew from his memory as well as his pilot's log book and scrap books kept over the years. Additional information came from interviews with former MHAs Tom Hickey and Bill Callahan. The following publications were consulted when necessary:

A History of the Royal Canadian Air Force by Christopher Shores, Bison Books copyright 1984

The internet site of Scandanavian Airlines at http://www.sas.se/sas/aboutus/history_brief.htm

The Little Airline That Could by Marsh Jones, Creative Publishers copyright 1998

The Transport Canada Canadian Civil Aircraft Register web site at: http://www.tc.gc.ca/

Janes World Aircraft Recognition Handbook, 5th edition, copyright Derek Wood 1992.

The Encyclopedia of World Aircraft, Prospero Books, copyright 1997.

INDEX

A
Aeronca 22
Akerman, Hewlett 42
American Consulate 15
American Overseas Airways 21
Argentia 11
Atlantic Airways 73, 75
Atlantic Aviation 58, 59
Automatic direction finder 39, 40
Avco-Lycoming 46
Aztec Aviation 71, 72

B
Barnes, Herb 12
Beaver (aircraft) 35, 37, 38, 39, 40, 41, 43, 47, 53, 73
Beechcraft 1, 4, 46, 62, 68, 69
Bell (helicopters) 67, 75, 76
Bergarud, Tom Dr. 34
Boeing 24, 31
Bragg, Hattie 21
Bridger, Neil 46, 47, 61
British Overseas Airways Corp. 18
Buchans 34
Burke, Carl 23
Butrym, John 42

C
California 24, 25
Callahan, William 56, 58, 59, 60
Canadian Helicopters 21, 77

Canso (aircraft) 41, 43, 44, 47, 48
Caribou, The 12
Cartwright 39
Cashin, Richard 29
Cessna 22, 24, 31, 42, 47, 68
C-FGNL 1, 3
Chicago 25
Christian Brothers 9
Clarenville 29
Collingwood, Tom 71, 73
Cooper, Debbie 21
Cooper, Royal 32, 37, 43, 51
Copeland, John 15, 16

D
Daily News, The 66
DC-3 (aircraft) 39, 49
DC-4 (aircraft) 23, 24
Deadman's Pond 37, 38
Dearin, Charlie 25
de Havilland 17, 37, 48
Deer Lake 1, 2, 21, 50
Dennison Mines 68
Dobbin, Craig 65, 73
Dunlop, Ian 18

E
Eastern Provincial Airways 29, 31, 35, 37, 39, 42, 43, 44, 46, 51, 58, 59, 60, 79
English, Bill 26
Evening Telegram 26
Executive Helicopters 75

F
Field Aviation 68
First Air 70
Flying Tiger Line 22, 23
Found (aircraft) 46, 47
Fowler, Bob 49, 51
Frankfurt, Germany 22, 23
French, John 44

G
Gander 3, 17, 18, 21, 22, 27, 37, 38, 39, 43, 50, 51, 54, 56
Goobie, Charlie 1, 4, 6, 7
Government Air Services 59
Government of Newfoundland and Labrador 1

H
Hamilton, Ontario 27
Harbour Deep 39
Henley, Ted 18, 19
Hickey, Tom 1, 6
Holy Cross (school) 9, 12
Home, The 11, 12
Hurricane (aircraft) 9, 10
Hutton, Noel 67, 75

J
Janes, Jack 17
Jones, Marsh 51

K
Kieley, Bill 12

L
Labrador Airways 69
Laurel, Gunnar 35, 36
Link trainer 43
Lush, Tom 65, 66
Lycoming 27

M
Malone, Mary Elizabeth 11, 13
March, Robert 79, 80
Maritime Central Airways 23
Mary's Harbour 39, 42
Monkman, Bill 27, 28
Montgomery, Bernard 54, 55, 56
Montreal 23, 24
Moore, Ralph 29
Moores, Frank 65

N
Napa Valley 25
Neary, Steve 65, 66
Newfoundland Armature Works 25
Newfoundland Railway 11, 13

O
Oakland, Calif. 24, 25
Octagon Pond 31, 51, 56
Otter and Twin Otter (aircraft) 35, 37, 38, 40, 41, 43, 48, 49, 50, 51, 52, 54, 56, 62, 63, 79, 81

P
Paddy's Pond 51

Pan American Airways 18, 21
Paradise 31
Patey, Bert 69
Pearcey, Aiden 29
Pearcey, Charles, 12
Pearcey, Glen 21
Pearcey, William John 11, 12
Penny, Ron 47, 48, 61
Peters, Stuart 31, 32
Piper (aircraft) 22, 27, 31, 33, 37, 43, 71, 72
Placentia Bay 11
Port Union 21
Pratt & Whitney 41, 51

R
RAF 18
Ragged Harbour 38
Red Bay 39
Reinhold, Henning 16, 17
Rhein-Main airport 22
Roberts, Ed 61
Rousseau, Joe 1, 6, 7

S
San Francisco 25
Scandinavian Airways System 16, 17, 18
Sealand Helicopters 66
Shannon, Clint 51
Smallwood, Joesph 51, 52, 53, 54, 56, 57, 58, 59, 60, 81
Snow, Robert 71
Spitfire (aircraft) 9

Squires, Eli 71
St. Anthony 39
St. John's 1, 3, 5, 9, 10, 27, 20, 50, 51, 52, 56, 69, 70, 75
St. John's Flying Club 29
St. Pat's Hall 26
Stoyles, Brother Billy 10
Stratocruiser 24

T
Taylorcraft (aircraft) 18
Tiger Moth (aircraft) 17
Torbay 17, 25
Trans Ocean Airlines 24
Travis Air Force Base 25
Trudeau, Pierre 54, 55

U
Universal Helicopters 65

V
VHF (very high frequency) 40
Victoria Lake 34
VOR (very high frequency omni-directional range) 40

W
White Bay 39
Williamsport 46